101 Things Salespeople Do To Sabotage Success

Mark S. Loper

Richard Chang Associates, Inc.
Publications Division
Irvine, California

101 Stupid Things Salespeople Do To Sabotage Success

Mark S. Loper

Library of Congress Catalog Card Number
97-66240

© 1998, Richard Chang Associates, Inc.
Printed in the United States of America

All rights reserved. No part of this publication may be reproduced, stored in a retrieval system, or transmitted in any form or by any means—electronic, mechanical, photocopying, recording, or otherwise—without the prior written permission of the publisher.

ISBN 1-883553-95-4

Editors:	Bill Foster and Karen Johnson
Reviewer:	Shirley Codrey
Graphic Layout:	Christina Slater
Cover Design:	Dena Putnam

RICHARD CHANG ASSOCIATES

Richard Chang Associates, Inc.
Publications Division
15265 Alton Parkway, Suite 300
Irvine, CA 92618
(800) 756-8096   (714) 727-7477
Fax (714) 727-7007
www.richardchangassociates.com

About The Author

Mark S. Loper is a sales professional with a Fortune 500 company and has over two decades of diverse selling experience. Under duress, he admits to collecting all 101 Stupid Things from his own mistakes and, actually, still has enough material for another ten books. Mark is also a writer who specializes in humor and has written advertising copy, TV and film scripts, a newspaper column, and corporate comedy. Mark still has those unsettling days when he's constantly rejected and no one appreciates his sparkling, unusual, droll, engaging, delightful, wonderful, and keen sense of humor. And that's from his family before he even leaves the house.

Acknowledgments

This book could not have been written without input from my family, friends, and colleagues. I'd like to thank my wife June, Tom Borchard, George Schmidt, Bill Foster, and, of course, Brendan and Bridget, who have always been my toughest critics.

Table of Contents

Introduction viii

1. Prospecting & Qualifying 1
#1 Maybe I Can Get Through With A Tank
#2 Think Big, Act Small
#3 Eat, Sleep, & Prospect
#4 When Bigger Is Better
#5 Mingle And Tingle
#6 We Don't Need No Stinkin' Budgets!
#7 Maybe Our Voice Mails Can Meet For Lunch
#8 There's Gold In Them Thar Calls!
#9 Where's That Mother Lode?

2. Cold Calling & Getting The Appointment 13
#10 Over Their Heads And Off With Yours!
#11 Right Building, Wrong Office
#12 Let Me Outta This Place!
#13 Let's Get Together And Shoot Some Pool
#14 Don't Call Me, I Won't Call You
#15 Just Let Me Put These Paper Clips In Order

3. Relationships & People Skills 21
#16 Attack Is Not A Good Tact
#17 Politics Make For Stupid Bedfellows
#18 Be Like Gumby (That's Flexible, Not Green)
#19 Arrogance Goeth Before The Fall
#20 Fork On The Left, Tie In The Soup
#21 I Love You The Same, That's Why I Married You Both
#22 Loose Lips Sink Ships (And Stupid Salespeople)
#23 It's Like Trying To Get Blood From A Vampire
#24 Surrounded By Imbeciles
#25 Rapoor: Tough To Spell And Important To Master

#26 I Didn't Do Anything, It's All Her Fault!
#27 If At First She Doesn't Like You . . . Well, She Probably Never Will
#28 Brews And Bruises
#29 Those Customers Think They Know Everything

4. Knowing Your Prospect 37
#30 What's Your Line?
#31 How Low Can You Go?
#32 Show And Tell
#33 I'll Take Three Widgets And Did I Mention My Swiss Bank Account?
#34 Sum Up Your Life In One Sentence Or Less
#35 If I Scratch Your Back, Don't You Stab Mine
#36 They Don't Call Them Competitors For Nothing
#37 She Can Do More Than Accessorize
#38 So The Controller Is Connected To The Thigh Bone
#39 All I Need Is Product Literature And A Crystal Ball

5. Presentations & Meetings 49
#40 Familiarity Breeds Contempt
#41 Have You Ever Heard Of Murphy's Law?
#42 Where Am I?
#43 I've Got The Handouts, Who's Got The Cue Cards?
#44 Yes, We Have No Agenda
#45 When "Demo" Is A Four-Letter Word
#46 Pupils; Retinas; Corneas; Oh, My!
#47 Do Butterflies Have Teeth?
#48 I'd Recognize That Voice Anywhere
#49 When Four-Letter Words Kill That Four-Letter Word Called Sale!
#50 The Good, The Bad, And The Stupid
#51 Maybe I Should Make It Multiple Choice

6. Handling Objections & Getting Referrals 63
#52 Is It The Mind That Goes First?
#53 But I Thought Price And Cost Were Synonyms
#54 Ask And Ye Shall Receive
 (Well, Only If Ye Have Answered Thy Objections)
#55 Now I Have To Schedule A Seance
#56 Why Don't They Just Shut Up And Buy?

7. Closing The Sale 71
#57 And Take Your Ring Too!
#58 Sticks & Stones May Break My Bones, But Those Words Really Kill Me
#59 Cross My Heart . . . Oh, You're Right, It Is On The Other Side
#60 Etiquette & Iterate
#61 Is Putting His Head Between His Legs A Buying Signal?
#62 Where's A Decision Maker When You Need One?
#63 I Know It's Just In From Paris, But It Still Makes Me Look Stupid
#64 What Will It Take For You To Buy This Tool Right Now, Huh, Huh, Huh!?
#65 All I Asked For Was Two Front Teeth
#66 Making A List And Checking It Twice
#67 Tell Him I'm Out And Moved To Brazil

8. After The Sale & After The Call 85
#68 Sold: Going, Going, Gone . . .
#69 When No Follow-Up Is A Foul Up
#70 I Shall Return (Except Not During Office Hours)
#71 Heads You Pay, Tails We Split It
#72 Elevators Have Ears Too
#73 And I Even Took Her To Lunch!
#74 Do Partners Need Pre-Nuptial Agreements?
#75 Should It Be Sincerely, Regards, Or Hugs And Kisses?

9. Your Image & Doing The Right Thing......95

#76 First Impressions
#77 Send In The Clowns
#78 A Group Photo Of Myself
#79 Lunch On The Rocks, Please
#80 He Orders 20 Lots And You Get 20 Years
#81 Talk, Talk, Talk And Watch The Order Walk
#82 Kiss, Bow, or Shake Hands?
#83 As Simple As 1-2-4
#84 I Know! I Know! I Know! Well, Maybe I Don't!
#85 Undress For Success
#86 Questions? Not Me, I'm Selling!

10. Time Management & Goal Setting 109

#87 Cleveland At Ten, Seattle At Two
#88 Should I Or Shouldn't I Use A Comma?
#89 Look Who Drove Up. Quick, Put Up The "Gone Fishin' " Sign!
#90 And I Don't Even Own Stock In The Phone Company!
#91 Pride Goeth Before The No Sale
#92 Not Another Bull In A China Shop!

11. Other Stupid Stuff 117

#93 The Rocky Road (With Two Scoops) I Can Handle
#94 Sorry, I'm A Day Late, But It's Not My Fault
#95 Been There, Done That
#96 Oh, My Aching Back!
#97 Aloha, Job!
#98 I Cannot Tell A Lie, Except On My Expense Report
#99 Maybe I Should Just Be A Sales Manager
#100 Is That A Participle Dangling From Your Gerund?
#101 I'm Finished Washing Your Car Boss, Anything Else?

Summary 129

Introduction

> *"The gift of being a salesperson is that we have the opportunity to make that choice everyday, each time we are face to face with a customer."*
> **E. Thomas Behr Ph.D.**

All of us are salespeople. Some of us may not want to admit it because we have professions that are not defined as sales. But what about those individuals in customer service or the company receptionist that first greets and then reroutes incoming calls? And let's look outside business. What are you doing when you meet someone you like? What are you doing when you take your children to school and meet their teachers for the first time? What about when the police pull you over for speeding? Okay, well, maybe that's begging. But what is it when you're looking for that preferential treatment at a hotel or you're meeting with the taxman? You're selling yourself! We do it all the time! And we're constantly getting rejected. It's a miracle we're not all in therapy.

Even the professions that might disdain selling involve selling. Aren't doctors, lawyers, teachers, and professional athletes also selling? Of course they are. And we're not talking autographs. These professionals have to sell, in their own way, to their own audience.

And even if you're adamant that you never, ever sell, then aren't you being sold to? Do you own a car? A house? Clothes that the salesperson said look terrific on you? And you just know he'd say the same thing if he was fitting Humpty Dumpty. Wouldn't it help you in the selling process if you had an idea of what was going through the mind of that salesperson?

This book can help make that constant part of your life easier; whether you're in business sales or just everyday, getting-thru-life sales. It's a reference tool designed for browsing, and certainly for enjoying.

We'll also improve your selling skills by highlighting what you may be doing wrong, but more importantly, offer some direction as to how you can do it right. It's all there in black and white with funny cartoons. All the answers you've ever been searching for are just ahead. So read on, and we hope you giggle now and then, chuckle, and maybe even laugh at loud.

Of course, we realize how difficult it is to evoke a hearty laugh, but we're a confident bunch. And we always think it's far easier to learn when you can also look at the humorous side of your own behavior. In other words, this book is filled with helpful hints, ideas, and suggestions that will help you become a better salesperson. After all, there are at least 101 success strategies listed for you to begin to use on your very next sales call.

So, have a good time with *101 Stupid Things Salespeople Do To Sabotage Success* and don't be surprised at how much of this book applies to your life. We feel this book will help you become better at what you are, and isn't that what we're always trying to do in life?

Chapter 1
Prospecting & Qualifying

#1 Maybe I Can Get Through With A Tank

You've made numerous phone calls to a top-level executive, but to no avail. Her secretary is a master at screening all callers; she doesn't return any of your calls; and though a terrific prospect, you're ready to give up.

What's Wrong?

- Picking up the phone for this prospect may be a waste of time.

- Repeated calling makes you look like a pest, and pests are not professional.

- If you ever do get through, your frustration could reveal itself in your conversation.

- Giving up is not part of a successful salesperson's mantra.

- You probably shouldn't open with "Hey, what's goin' down and how 'bout passin' me on to the Big Unit!?"

Some Success Strategies:

Try calling before the secretary comes in, during her lunch hour, or after she leaves at the end of the day. The executive may just pick up her own phone. Write a letter suggesting a time when you will call. Obviously, try to appeal to this "future client" with tantalizing bait in the letter. Send her a telegram. Be creative. Refrain from following her home.

#2 Think Big, Act Small

You're so excited about your new sales position that you just can't wait to present to the largest accounts in your territory. You may stumble and not be sure of all the benefits for your key prospects, but you'll overwhelm them with your enthusiasm.

What's Wrong?

- 📣 Enthusiasm will not close the sale.

- 📣 Initially, you won't have any credibility with the large prospects.

- 📣 You're not willing to make less grievous mistakes with smaller clients.

- 📣 It's no different outside the office; you can't wait to raft Niagara Falls.

- 📣 Your rookie mistakes could cause irreparable damage to major accounts.

Some Success Strategies:

Call on the smaller accounts and ask questions. Begin by asking easy questions of the prospect. Uncover objections and try overcoming them. Throw yourself into the sales arena and drink in the experience, but be patient. Moderate your enthusiasm. Before you approach the large, complex opportunities, be certain your confidence level is appropriate to the sales call. You want to be able to walk back into those doors later. And leave your pom-poms at home.

#3 Eat, Sleep, & Prospect

You feel terrific since you closed that last sale. Everything was done right and you exceeded your quota for the month. The only thing you didn't do, unfortunately, was prospect during this time.

What's Wrong?

- There's no new business in the pipeline.

- You quickly find yourself stressed.

- New monthly demands cause you to neglect follow-up and not provide support for existing clients.

- You start selling with an attitude of desperation.

- You also forgot your wife's birthday, and you just realized she's not home because you forgot to pick her up at the airport last night.

Some Success Strategies:

Always be prospecting. Always be reading, listening, and looking for leads. Set aside time each day or week to just prospect. This means picking up the phone, sending out sales letters or letters of introduction, or knocking on doors. Ask your existing clients for referrals. And maybe for a few, good marriage counselors. You must always be planting seeds for the future harvest.

#4 When Bigger Is Better

Though you're closing at a high percentage, you're still knocking yourself out calling on small accounts. You soon realize you'll never make any money this way.

What's Wrong?

☆ While you're closing the small accounts, your competition is closing the big ones.

☆ The payback or return on selling time is abysmal.

☆ In not pursuing the larger accounts, you're starting to lose your confidence.

☆ You're missing a great opportunity to make much more money.

☆ In starting to think big, you put on 146 pounds.

Some Success Strategies:

It's good to think big. You'll discover that larger accounts often are less trouble than smaller accounts. Start with mid-sized firms to bolster your confidence and prevent any sale-stopping mistakes at the higher levels. Call to the top and recognize the inherent complexities of a larger prospect. Study the organization and be informed. The larger accounts are called on more frequently, mandating that you be more polished. You'll have to be more creative and better prepared. The payoff will make the extra preparation worthwhile.

#5 Mingle And Tingle

Even though you're attending numerous industry luncheons and functions you still never go out of your way to meet people. You convince yourself you're not an introvert, you figure you can just call them when you have to.

What's Wrong?

☞ Opportunities to discover new business are being missed.

☞ You appear introverted and unapproachable.

☞ Networking is an alien concept to you.

☞ Your finger isn't on the true "pulse" of the business if you're not actually talking, face-to-face, with the players.

☞ You're not taking advantage of meeting your associates on a social level.

☞ And you wonder why you're not married.

Some Success Strategies:

Network, network, network. Introduce yourself to as many people as you can at these functions. Pass out your business card and, like a good salesperson, ask questions. Find out what the person does and who they work with; see how this connection might benefit you. Volunteer to be on industry committees and participate in workshops or other activities. Be as visible as possible.

#6 We Don't Need No Stinkin' Budgets!

You've put a lot of time into identifying a prospect's needs, meeting the right people, and presenting your solutions. They say they love your product, but now they're not sure if they can afford it.

What's Wrong?

$ You didn't determine up front if there was a budget for your solution.

$ If you'd known their budgetary limitations initially, you could have crafted a more feasible proposal.

$ You can't convince your prospect to charge it to their credit card.

$ The commitment to truly solving their problem was never made by the prospect.

Some Success Strategies:

One of the most important qualifying questions in any buying situation is determining how much the prospect has to invest. You don't want to waste your time trying to sell a luxury car to someone who's only looking for a test drive. Ask the prospect what they're looking for and, in essence, what their budget parameters are. Be cautious if the reply consists of, "Oh, we'll spend as much as it takes," or "The decision will be made quickly." See, this sounds suspiciously like the government. Your sales solution must be molded to answer customer needs, but it must also fit neatly into their fiscal plans.

#7 Maybe Our Voice Mails Can Meet For Lunch

It seems everyone has voice mail today, but when you leave messages, your calls are rarely returned. When you finally do contact the party, you can't help but be extremely annoyed.

What's Wrong?

- This negative attitude will be conveyed to the prospect.
- You're wasting a lot of time leaving messages that rarely get returned.
- By not making contact, you're not making sales.
- You're not coping well with today's technology.
- In retaliation, you've stopped returning calls, answering your doorbell, and you're even ignoring those darn shrieking fire alarms.

Some Success Strategies:

Plan what you're going to say and keep your message short and simple. Speak clearly, spell names, and emphasize key words. Try not to speak too fast and don't try to sell. You don't want to give the person a reason to avoid calling you back. Be sincere with your message, and say nothing about Amway. If you're going to be in and out, give the prospect a choice of times when you'll be available to take his call.

#8 There's Gold In Them Thar Calls!

You know you should make an effort to set aside time to prospect, but you're too busy following up on current business. You'll get around to it sometime.

What's Wrong?

☎ You're certainly not planning well.

☎ After you've caught up on your current business, you won't have any imminent sales in the pipeline.

☎ Management may be concerned about your uneven sales activity.

☎ You've done the same thing in looking for a spouse, and now you're 56 with no muscle tone and no matrimony.

☎ When you finally do prospect it will be out of necessity fueled by desperation.

Some Success Strategies:

Set aside time each day for prospecting and try to make it a game with achievable goals. Be prepared with a list of names to call, making the calls brief, and making as many calls as possible. Work without interruption, be organized, and consider calling at off-times to improve your chances of making contact. Most importantly, don't stop. Remember, the objective of prospecting is to get a meeting. And after you've done all this in trying to get a date, then do the same for business.

#9 Where's That Mother Lode?

You're excited about your product, your training, and now you're hungry and ready to go. But where do you get your prospects? Maybe you'll just start dialing numbers from the phone book.

What's Wrong?

- The warm market, the prospects you already know, are being neglected.
- You're facing immediate rejection which can undercut your confidence.
- Your company's sales training process is deficient.
- You won't have a chance to polish your sales presentation with random calls made to unknown names in the phone book.
- It'll be difficult getting referrals from the cold market.
- You practice by calling your mother and she won't take your call.

Some Success Strategies:

Talk to your existing clients, friends, and people you already know, including business associates, first. If you have a customer list, go through it and learn why these people bought the first time and where they might be now in the buying cycle. Talk to salespeople in different professions who understand your position. You might even try the 5-foot rule where you strike up a conversation with anyone within five feet of you to determine if this individual is a viable prospect. By this time you'll be much more comfortable and when you pick up the phone you'll know what you're looking for, and what questions to ask.

Chapter 2

Cold Calling & Getting The Appointment

#10 Over Their Heads And Off With Yours!

You made an appointment with your prospect's boss because you couldn't get a decision from your prospect.

What's Wrong?

- ☠ Any future working relationship with your prospect has been impaired.

- ☠ Your prospect's boss may resent your intrusion.

- ☠ A very uncomfortable business atmosphere has been created.

- ☠ Even if a sale is made, the shunned prospect can hinder post-sale progress.

- ☠ The prospect has an overprotective brother getting out of prison; he was in for randomly assaulting salespeople.

Some Success Strategies:

Discuss with your prospect what difficulties there may be in making this decision. Ask, tactfully, if there is anyone else within the organization that can assist you. For example: "Who besides yourself will be involved in making a decision to move forward?" Try to determine if the prospect is truly your ally. Mention your participation in Free-A Felon Day. Probe for other objections. Only go above this individual if you have nothing to lose, and always be aware of the possible consequences.

#11 Right Building, Wrong Office

You need to see the marketing director of a large firm, but you find it far easier to get to the purchasing manager. So you make an appointment with her!

What's Wrong?

- You're calling on the wrong person.

- Purchasing will be alienated, weakening your chances of getting to the marketing level.

- You're trying to sell up, instead of down.

- The purchasing manager was out and you ended up meeting with a transient at the bus stop.

Some Success Strategies:

Be more creative in calling on the marketing director by perhaps, sending a telegram. It's also much easier to sell down rather than up. Call on the marketing director's superior, even if it's the president. Then, if you're referred down, you're right where you want to be. Now, you're calling under the auspices of this director's boss and you'll surely find an audience.

#12 Let Me Outta This Place!

You can't stand making cold calls. You *stare* at the phone like it's going to attack, and then make up as many excuses as possible to postpone the inevitable.

What's Wrong?

- Every minute you procrastinate, you could be losing a sale.
- You can't overcome this fear unless you face it.
- When you finally make a call, you shout "Hallelujah" after getting a busy signal.
- Perhaps you're just not the prospecting type.

Some Success Strategies:

Just pick up the phone and call. Don't expect to be perfect with your pitch, but do expect to be rejected. It's all part of the selling process. Schedule a number of calls to make before a designated time and then reward yourself when you reach that number. Though taking the rest of the day off might be counterproductive. Challenge yourself on this level, and put the actual selling, or getting the appointment, in a secondary position. Take the pressure off and relax. Now your prospect will hear the "real" you, and you'll sound much more convincing and credible.

#13 Let's Get Together And Shoot Some Pool

You're having a difficult time securing appointments. The prospect seems interested in your verbal proposal, but when you mention setting up an appointment for about an hour, you find yourself talking to a dial tone.

What's Wrong?

- An hour is too long.

- Appointments are for doctors, dentists, and auto shops; all expensive and painful.

- You're not asking the right "checking" questions.

- In asking for a face-to-face you're using the wrong terminology.

- Now you're including Dial Tone, Inc. on your prospect list.

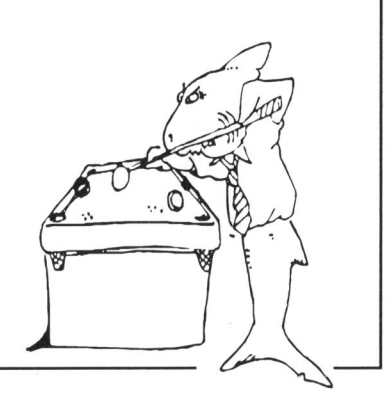

Some Successful Strategies:

Don't ask for an hour on the initial call. Try to keep it brief and even ask for less time than necessary. If the prospect is interested, you'll find yourself with more than enough time. The word "appointment" may have a harsh connotation; perhaps try "get together." The key is offering the prospect something she wants to hear more about. Stimulate her interest, but don't tell everything. Let her know you have proof. And you want the money in small, unmarked bills.

#14 Don't Call Me, I Won't Call You

You've worked hard to get a key appointment and when you call the day before to confirm, your contact apologizes and says something has "come up." He asks if you wouldn't mind calling next week to schedule another appointment.

What's Wrong?

- You may not get another appointment.

- That something that has "come up" may be a meeting with your competitor.

- The prospect doesn't find your appointment too important.

- You weren't clear enough with your prospect when you first made the appointment.

Some Success Strategies:

Send a quick note a week before your meeting confirming your appointment. Convey the significance of your "getting together" and be on time so an excuse can't be made to not see you. Once you arrive, there may be a need, but even more importantly, there is now an obligation on the prospect's part to see you. Do confirm if substantial travel is involved, if you're assembling a team for the meeting, or if your prospect is named Slick.

#15 Just Let Me Put These Paper Clips In Order

You have become the master of organization. Your files are in order, your pencils sharpened, and your desk is clean. The problem is, you've been organizing for two weeks now.

What's Wrong?

- You're not selling.

- Just the thought of selling has you petrified.

- You haven't had enough training.

- Your underwear drawer is still a mess.

- The competition is taking your business.

Some Success Strategies:

Take a deep breath and plunge in. With every new sales effort you must expect to feel *stupid* (there's that word again) at times. You'll also be emotionally bruised, but that's all part of the process for a successful salesperson. Think *positive!* and *attack!* and grab that phone and know you are good! Don't worry about the consequences because you know how to sell and even more importantly, you're reading this book! Whew!

Chapter 3
Relationships & People Skills

#16 Attack Is Not A Good Tact

Your prospect praises your competition, and you respond by harshly criticizing them.

What's Wrong?

- You're making the prospect look bad by disagreeing with them.

- It's negative selling.

- It's unprofessional behavior.

- It sounds a little childish when you chant, "Na na nanana, bet they can't do this!"

- The competition's weaknesses won't be uncovered now.

Some Success Strategies:

If your prospect compliments your competition, agree with the assessment. Try to discover what your competitor does well and in what areas their performance could be improved. Ask if he's aware they watch afternoon talk shows. Your job is to determine how you can better fill this prospect's needs.

#17 Politics Make For Stupid Bedfellows

You have strong opinions and voice many of your beliefs with your prospects, especially when it comes to politics.

What's Wrong?

- 📢 Alienating your prospect is a definite possibility.
- 📢 Your strong views could kill the sale.
- 📢 Making many friends in your own company will be difficult.
- 📢 You sound ignorant.
- 📢 You could also be politically incorrect.

Some Success Strategies:

Keep your opinions to yourself and denounce nothing. Never take sides on creationism versus evolution. Speak more freely only when you know your prospect well and the situation allows for it. Ask leading questions and see where the replies carry you and then formulate your position in relation to the prospect's. Save your political opinions for an Internet chat room.

#18 Be Like Gumby (That's Flexible, Not Green)

You're the enthusiastic type of salesperson that gets along with almost anyone—except for this latest buyer, who seems cold and only interested in profits. You're ready to move on to another prospect that will laugh at your jokes.

What's Wrong?

- Your personality is at odds with that of the prospect's.
- Too much of yourself was revealed too quickly.
- The "authority" personality was not recognized.
- You failed to adjust your approach to this type of personality.
- And she doesn't care about that picture of your cute kid either.

Some Success Strategies:

Ask questions and try to identify the different buying mind sets: authoritative, amiable, ego, grouchy, etc. For instance, with the authoritative figure you must demonstrate competence. Model yourself after the decision maker and be aware of what personality styles may clash. Try to find something out about the person you'll be calling on. Be flexible without appearing fake.

#19 Arrogance Goeth Before The Fall

You're so good. Besides being a great salesperson, you also let everyone know it, including your associates, friends, customers, prospects, and mailman.

What's Wrong?

- You're insufferable.
- Prospects prefer confidence, not arrogance.
- Customers will not want to continue doing business with you.
- Your sales will soon react inversely to the size of your ego.
- When you need support from your colleagues you won't find it.
- Soon you won't have any friends, but you will have tons of junk mail.

Some Successful Strategies:

You have to make a conscious effort to keep your mouth shut and think about what you might say. Put yourself in the position of the person you're speaking to. You need to modify your behavior, compliment others whenever possible, and recognize their worth. Listen and look up the word humility. Practice it. Try sending this message to your mailman too. Just don't mark it fragile.

#20 Fork On The Left, Tie In The Soup

You're having dinner with a major prospect, and aside from sliding food into your mouth with a butter knife and talking with your mouth full, everything seems to be going well.

What's Wrong?

- That new spot on your prospect's tie looks suspiciously like your salad dressing.

- Your dinner partner is repulsed by your actions.

- The terrible impression you're making doesn't reflect well on your company.

- If the prospect sees little difference between competitors, your outrageous table manners could tip the scales the other way.

- Your lobster entree hasn't even been served yet.

Some Success Strategies:

You must teach yourself how to eat properly in a restaurant. Read a book on good table manners or take a class on dinner etiquette. If, for example, you're not sure where to put the spoon from your bisque, follow the lead of your dinner companion. If international travel is on the horizon, research is a must. Go out to eat with friends that don't eat with their fingers and have them critique your style. By the way, that spoon goes on the saucer beneath the bowl. And wipe your mouth.

#21 I Love You The Same, That's Why I Married You Both

You've been passing on more leads and going out of your way for one of your customers, but now another customer that's observed this preferential treatment is asking for some of the same. Since you don't have as good a personal relationship with this neglected customer, you simply make up excuses why you can't help them as much. In other words, you fib.

What's Wrong?

- The relationship with the customer now asking for help will be weakened.

- This neglected and demanding customer may take their complaint to your upper management.

- As word spreads about this favoritism your reputation in the industry will suffer.

- You haven't been very fair. And you're lying.

- Now you're feeling so guilty you have your therapist on speed dial.

Some Success Strategies:

Attempt to show fairness in dealing with all your customers. It's true you'll have customers that you favor, but any favoritism should only be revealed on a personal level. Both customers deserve equal opportunities to share in your expertise. You may choose to deal with one customer because of their unique market skills, but at least in this instance, your choice can be supported.

#22 Loose Lips Sink Ships (And Stupid Salespeople)

You're socializing with a prospect and after having a few drinks, you become quite talkative. You tell your companion about some of the rumors, critical and damaging rumors, that are circulating about the prospect's competition.

What's Wrong?

- Your discretion is no longer a consideration.

- The prospect will worry about you spilling his company secrets if she ever did business with you.

- In telling these rumors, which are not absolute truths, the prospect will wonder if you're also stretching the truth in trying to make this sale.

- The prospect may have friends with the competition and will resent your implications.

- You're making less money from your job than you are selling gossip to the tabloids.

Some Success Strategies:

Discretion is something all companies value, and you need to practice this if you expect to be anyone's business partner. Don't tell tales about competitors because your prospect is probably closer to the truth than you are. If your prospect tells you something revealing then file it away; don't try to match it with your own secret or rumor. Discuss the competition from a professional position; sharing information that is in the public domain. Think before you open your mouth and recognize the discomfort of sticking a foot in it.

#23 It's Like Trying To Get Blood From A Vampire

You're a tenacious salesperson and you won't take no for an answer. Now the prospect won't return your phone calls, and the last time you did talk, he hung up on you.

What's Wrong?

- Everyone can't be sold.

- Other opportunities to meet with people that want to buy are being missed.

- Your obnoxious reputation will spread throughout the industry and affect future prospects.

- You're calling a prospect that has actually been dead for a year.

- This kind of behavior will make you more enemies than friends.

Some Success Strategies:

Learn to walk away from a sale that simply isn't going to happen and put your time to more productive use. If you've answered all objections and the prospect still won't budge, then you should. Never forget that selling is a numbers game. Don't allow yourself to get too close to a possible sale because of the emotional fallout if it doesn't materialize. Think of all the tissue you'll save.

#24 Surrounded By Imbeciles

Every lost sale is blamed on: poor technical support, mediocre products, thick-headed prospects, unfair territory alignment, and even weak management. You also let everyone know how you feel.

What's Wrong?

☹ You're immature and can't take responsibility for your own actions.

☹ No one will appreciate or want to listen to your carping and complaining.

☹ Everything you say reflects badly on your company.

☹ You'll quickly find yourself without allies or friends.

☹ And also without a job.

Some Success Strategies:

Improve your attitude. Look hard at the competition and determine if their products are actually better and objectively assess your territory's potential. Meet with management to see where your career path may lead. Tally your results and if you still can't find anything positive about what you're doing or where you're going, then look elsewhere. There are always opportunities for whiny, self-serving ingrates in politics. However, if you decide to stay, it's your duty and responsibility to provide advice and suggestions to improve upon the shortcomings of your company's products and/or services.

#25 Rapoor: Tough To Spell And Important To Master

You're getting appointments, asking all the right questions, and giving presentations. Maybe you're not bonding too well with the prospect, but everything else is going well and yet you're still not getting the business.

What's Wrong?

- All the objections are not being uncovered.
- You don't understand the value of relationships and a mutual level of trust has not been established.
- You may be deficient in social skills.
- Selling that demands bonding between the prospect and the salesperson may not be your strength.
- You think rapport is some kind of street music sung by sailors on leave.

Some Success Strategies:

Rapport is one of the most important elements of any sales call and it usually leads to respect. Establish a relationship and you'll uncover objections easily and shorten the sales process. Rapport has to be developed naturally, through a common interest or a meshing of personalities. Ask numerous questions to find out as much as you can about the business and the buyer. Be able to delve into subject matter that may have nothing to do with business, but has something to do with the prospect. Read different magazines, newspapers, and books to diversify your knowledge base.

#26 I Didn't Do Anything, It's All Her Fault!

Sales associates are working for you, and whenever a prospect or customer has a problem, you simply blame it on one of them.

What's Wrong?

☞ A wedge is being driven between you and your associates.

☞ Your associates will be less conscientious and your customer support will suffer.

☞ Customers will think little of you when the truth gets out.

☞ You're setting a terrible example.

☞ Integrity, strength of character, and guts are foreign to you.

Some Success Strategies:

If there's a problem, solve it as expeditiously as possible. If the fault is yours, own up to it in a forthright manner. Be mature about taking the blame. You don't want to lose your privileges or be grounded. If one of your associates makes the mistake, then have them get back to the customer with the appropriate apology. You don't want the customer focusing on what's wrong, but rather on what's right, by how well you rectified what was temporarily amiss.

#27 If At First She Doesn't Like You . . . Well, She Probably Never Will

First impressions don't concern you much because you think you always ask the right questions and give brilliant presentations.

What's Wrong?

✗ It will be harder to get good answers for those questions if you haven't made a good impression.

✗ The presentation stage will not be reached very often.

✗ This prospect won't be giving you any referrals.

✗ You're not approaching each account like a sales professional.

Some Success Strategies:

It's a good idea to try to get the prospect to like you and your organization. They'll relax and share more of their concerns with you if they're comfortable with your presence. Be cordial and pleasant and your prospect will probably respond in kind. Smile deeply and make eye contact during that initial meeting. But don't overdo the eye contact. People feel uncomfortable if they think they're being hypnotized. Greet them and shake hands when it's appropriate. Don't be too familiar as in calling a prospect by their first name if they've introduced themselves by Mr. or Ms. Be affable and respectful.

#28 Brews And Bruises

You're ambitious, aggressive, and demanding. You're also rude when dealing with your sales manager's secretary.

What's Wrong?

- You have no idea what the secretary is telling your boss and how much harm your behavior can cause.

- The secretary may have considerable influence around the office with other vital personnel.

- That report you needed typed by Friday is now mysteriously "lost."

- That pipeline for inside information has run dry.

- If you ever become a manager, you'll never find a secretary to work for you.

- Besides having someone taste your food before you eat it, now someone has to sip your coffee.

Some Success Strategies:

Treat the office staff with as much respect as you would customers. Ask questions that show you genuinely care. Respond to their queries and remember their birthdays. If you do have communication problems, talk it through try to and resolve the issues. If the problem persists, don't ignore it. Discuss it with your manager and explain how this debacle is affecting your job.

#29 Those Customers Think They Know Everything

In talking with a prospect, you always find something to disagree about. You simply can't tolerate other views and you have to argue.

What's Wrong?

✓ Bonding is certainly not in your vocabulary.

✓ Your reputation will always precede you and lead you nowhere.

✓ You won't have to concern yourself with follow-up calls.

✓ The integrity of your employer will suffer.

✓ You're too old to start a new career in the military.

Some Success Strategies:

You may want to defend your point of view, but discretion is the path to sales success. Listen to your prospect, but take note on how you'll eventually make them see your side of the issue. A new, big-screen TV is not an option. Initially, it's very important to develop a trustworthy relationship, and an adversarial one will only impair your chances of achieving a shared solution. When you've reached a level of mutual respect then you might disagree. Patience and self-control are truly beneficial to the sales process. Demonstrate that you really want this business and don't argue. Save that for your teenager.

Chapter 4

Knowing Your Prospect

#30 What's Your Line?

You're sitting across from the prospect and you open with, "So, you're one of the largest companies in the world, just what do you do, anyway?"

What's Wrong?

→ Research is obviously not your "thing."

→ Your interest in the organization and their overall business is suspect.

→ Your small talk skills need a little work.

→ Your next question is, "Okay, okay, it's still my turn, hmmm . . . okay, okay, so what's the cafeteria serving for lunch today?"

→ You've just destroyed your credibility.

Some Success Strategies:

Rule number one: Research! If they're a public company, do your research by requesting the organization's annual report or 10K. Check the Internet for information and search newspaper databases. Call the CEO's mother. She's usually listed. Talk to business contacts and friends that may have dealings with the organization. Simply find out as much as you can about your prospect because this is the first step to becoming this organization's partner.

#31 How Low Can You Go?

When meeting with a prospect you lead with "Whatever you're paying right now, we can beat it!"

What's Wrong?

- The prospect's other needs are being ignored because you're only selling price.

- You're not listening.

- It's offensive shoving price in the prospect's face.

- You're selling a commodity, not a service.

- This is not consultative selling, it's a proclamation.

- You sound like an irritating radio commercial.

Some Success Strategies:

Ask the prospect what he's looking for and what he needs. Don't necessarily give your selling price up-front, but determine what he expects for his purchase. Convince the prospect that the value for your solution is worth more than someone else's mere price. If, initially, he's not convinced then step through the benefit checklist again. If that doesn't work, tell him you're not leaving until he buys. Show him your sleeping bag. A successful sale will have the prospect wanting to do business with you. Cost will be secondary.

#32 Show And Tell

You show the prospect why he needs you by handing out your glossy brochure, your latest video, a CD-ROM with all your products on it, and a partridge in a pear tree. But you've forgotten to ask this interested party what he's really looking for.

What's Wrong?

- Expensive collateral material is being wasted.

- You're not willing to do the necessary preparation before calling on this account.

- You're not attempting to uncover the customer's needs.

- Darn, one of those videos you gave away was actually a home movie of your summer vacation to Disneyland.

Some Success Strategies:

Ask questions and listen. Think of yourself as a detective and probe. Find areas of concern, strategize possible solutions, and then present these solutions to your prospect. Distribute only what collateral information is necessary. Get that silly video back. And remember, this is support information. Brochures don't sell, people do.

#33 I'll Take Three Widgets And Did I Mention My Swiss Bank Account?

The buyer you're calling on is interested in what you're selling. But he's also interested in experiencing the pleasures of an ocean cruise and insinuates that your company can include his tickets in with the first order.

What's Wrong?

- It won't stop with an ocean cruise.

- If you give in, every other sizable order you write will require a kickback.

- You're placing yourself in a litigious position.

- You're compromising yourself ethically and morally.

- You're worried about his reaction when you offer him a paddle.

Some Success Strategies:

Explain that your company doesn't believe in doling out "favors," and neither do you. Again, sell your benefits. If he takes offense, then apologize and immediately report the incident to your superior. Then, after telling your wife, tell your sales manager. Be cognizant of your role as a business person, and try not to have that misinterpreted.

101 STUPID THINGS SALESPEOPLE DO TO SABOTAGE SUCCESS   41

#34 Sum Up Your Life In One Sentence Or Less

It's your first call on this account, and you have exactly five minutes to sell yourself and your organization to its CEO. You've got so much to tell her, you try to cover as much as you can.

What's Wrong?

- The CEO will be confused if you're passing out too much information in an aimless manner.

- The CEO won't be seeing her needs addressed.

- The prospect will see nothing different between your approach and that of your competition.

- As you're being escorted off the premises, you realize you probably shouldn't have made that comment about "women being better off in the kitchen."

- Five minutes goes by very, very, quickly.

Some Success Strategies:

Study your prospect and see where they might have a need for your products or services. Try to establish a "fit." Talk with those in the organization that work with the CEO and that know her likes, dislikes, and business philosophy. Tailor your presentation to those needs and offer the appropriate solutions. Rehearse and make every second count. Those five minutes are tremendously valuable, and if you've done your homework, they will pay off. Try not to get personal unless she calls you a name first.

#35 If I Scratch Your Back, Don't You Stab Mine

A prospect has given you a list of concerns to respond to and you practically burst out of his office to get on it. You don't have any commitment from the prospect and you didn't ask where your feedback will take you, but you're pretty sure it's closer to a sale.

What's Wrong?

- You're providing information without an agreement to get something in return.
- The prospect is taking advantage of your naivete.
- This legwork could be for a competitor.
- Enthusiasm has overcome your objectivity.
- You're working without any agreed upon objective.
- Now your stomach is growling as you order his lunch.

Some Success Strategies:

A sales situation is a give and give process. If the prospect asks for something and you can give it, you need to determine what they can give you in return. It's quid pro quo, and the prospect must understand this even if he didn't take Latin. If you can fulfill his needs, ask the prospect if this is enough for him to purchase your product. It's an effective checking question to determine if he's truly interested in doing business.

#36 They Don't Call Them Competitors For Nothing

In an effort to become more involved in your community, you decided to join a local business organization. However, during one of your meetings, you discover that two other members happen to work for your largest competitor. You introduce yourself and pretend they're not there.

What's Wrong:

- You have to be careful you don't give up any proprietary information.

- Your competitor may give you proprietary information, accidentally or intentionally, and expect you to do the same.

- You won't be able to share the "what I did at work today" story with one another.

- The purpose of a local business organization is to serve the community, not your competitor.

Some Success Strategies:

It's not a good idea to mix business with pleasure. Though it's not uncommon to be friends with a competitor, it's prudent to continue to deal with this person as simply another business professional. There are, obviously, different levels of competition and some have to be taken more seriously than others. Having an occasional lunch with a quasi-competitor to share industry information is not harmful, but caution still has to be on the menu. It can give you more than indigestion when you come back from the restroom and catch your lunchmate searching through your briefcase.

#37 She Can Do More Than Accessorize

You're selling to a man and his wife, and during the presentation you're giving all of your attention to the man.

What's Wrong?

- You appear sexist.
- The wife is being alienated.
- The wife will probably have a major influence on the decision.
- You still don't think women should vote.
- The husband could resent you for not addressing his wife.

Some Success Strategies:

In today's society, women make more buying decisions than ever before. Ask questions of both to find out their needs and demonstrate benefits while making eye contact with both. Try asking questions to determine who is the primary influencer for the purchase. When you discover who this is, focus on this person to gauge their buying interest. Even if you sense a bond between yourself and one of the parties, make a conscious effort to include the other in your discussions. Never ignore either person.

#38 So The Controller Is Connected To The Thigh Bone

While making calls on a large corporate account you have no idea how purchasing, marketing, sales, quality control, etc. interact or are connected to one another. You think your job is to get the sale, so you don't think it's important to know how the whole organization functions.

What's Wrong?

- You don't realize the influence individual departments can have on one another.

- You're not making a true effort to really know your customer.

- You may never know where the ultimate buying decision is made.

- If you start to lose the sale in one department, you won't know where to find support elsewhere in the organization.

- You even park in the CEO's reserved parking place, but think nothing of it since you're not calling on her.

- If there are corporate changes, you'll have very little idea what impact they'll have on you.

Some Success Strategies:

It's important to learn everything you can about your customers. Meet as many individuals from other departments as possible and try to find out each department's role in driving the business. Try to uncover what the needs of the major departments are in relevance to what you're selling.

#39 All I Need Is Product Literature And A Crystal Ball

During a sales call you don't feel the buyer is revealing her true objections. But, you're not going to bother with her "covert," or unstated concerns; you're going to proceed on just what she's saying.

What's Wrong?

★ You haven't handled all the objections, only the "overt" ones.

★ Many times the unstated objections or concerns are the most significant.

★ The solutions you provide will satisfy you, not your prospect.

★ You've asked the love of your life to marry you, ignoring the fact that, without you, she accepted a job on another continent.

★ All future dialogue will only be superficial, and you'll be skirting the substantial issues.

Some Success Strategies:

No sale will be made as long as "covert" concerns, or personal concerns, are left unaddressed. Some of these critical unasked questions might be: What is the buyer's personal risk? Will the buyer have more work? Is the buyer in deep thought or is she sound asleep? Will this solidify the buyer's position within the organization? Will this decision reflect positively on the buyer?· Read the hidden agenda and structure your sale to benefit not only the organization, but also the individual making the buying decision.

Chapter 5

Presentations & Meetings

#40 Familiarity Breeds Contempt

You're meeting a prospect for the first time, the conservative CEO of a mid-sized company. You greet him with a hearty, "Hey, Frank," and a terrific slap on the back.

What's Wrong?

👎 You're a bit presumptuous.

👎 The wrong tone has already been set for the meeting.

👎 Anyone else in the meeting will also feel offended by your treatment of their leader.

👎 The outcome of the sale leaves you blue.

👎 The outcome of the meeting leaves your prospect black and blue.

Some Success Strategies:

Determine the mood of the meeting by the behavior of the prospect. Ask questions in a carefully modulated manner, and if the prospect opens up, then you can open up, too. Unless he asks you to, don't call the CEO by his first name. Suppress your enthusiasm and earn his respect with your professional demeanor. Remember, this is difficult to do when you dislocate his shoulder.

#41 Have You Ever Heard Of Murphy's Law?

Suddenly, while you're putting on a spectacular multimedia presentation and your computer crashes, the LCD panel doesn't work, and you didn't think to bring any transparencies.

What's Wrong?

- This presentation reminds you of all that rewiring you just did for your mother-in-law.

- You didn't check all components before presenting.

- Backup materials were forgotten.

- You may be guilty of overkill.

Some Success Strategies:

Only use multimedia shows if necessary, and if overheads are sufficient, go no further. Keep it simple, but direct and effective. If videos or computers are necessary, check them more than once to be certain they're working properly. Get familiar with them and know where the stop button is on the VCR. Don't worry about setting the time, no one knows how to do that.

#42 Where Am I?

Your mind tends to wander when you're questioning a prospect. You seem preoccupied and inattentive.

What's Wrong?

- The customer perceives you're not interested.
- You're not focused on the situation before you.
- This sale is being lost before you've even started.
- You seem flaky.
- You're not setting a good example for your organization.
- Maybe those weren't your garden-variety mushrooms you had for lunch.

Some Success Strategies:

Try clearing your head before every call and then practice active listening. Do this by focusing on the prospect and what he's saying. Ask relevant questions and make eye contact. Take notes and nod your head when appropriate. Just don't snore.

#43 I've Got The Handouts, Who's Got The Cue Cards?

Your company prefers that you give presentations that are tightly scripted. Unfortunately, you don't memorize well, and the presentation is not going smoothly. You also forgot to set up the teleprompter.

What's Wrong?

- You sound nervous and don't inspire confidence in your audience.

- The presentation is mechanical and lacks spontaneity.

- Key points of the presentation are forgotten.

- The presentation is not crafted to your personality.

- You're so concerned with getting the script right, you don't notice the mood of the audience.

- The audience is getting restless and you notice some of them holding fruits and vegetables but lunch isn't for three hours!

Some Success Strategies:

Be yourself. Obviously, you must conform somewhat to the script, but attach your personal style to it. The audience will respond to you more than they will the material. Use your sense of humor but only if you have one. Be self-deprecating. Use a script as a springboard for key subject areas or to prompt reminders of important issues. You'll seem more comfortable, more relaxed, and more responsive to the audience if you perform within your own persona. If all this fails, prepare to duck.

#44 Yes, We Have No Agenda

After meeting with the prospect and sharing a lot of information, you walked away wondering what to do next.

What's Wrong?

- ? There was no specific agenda before the meeting.

- ? You haven't given yourself or the prospect a good reason to get back together.

- ? You don't know how to create an action plan.

- ? The prospect enjoyed your talk, has new information, but doesn't recognize your value.

- ? You're so confused you just took a taxi all the way back to the office before realizing that you drove to the prospect's place of business.

Some Success Strategies:

Have clear objectives for every call and know exactly what you want to accomplish. Listen to the prospect, but shape the discussion so you get your questions answered. Do not offer specific solutions until they're paramount to the closing of the sale. Be an *asset* for the prospect. Too often we're just the first syllable.

#45 When "Demo" Is A Four-Letter Word

You aren't prepared for your demonstration, and the frustrated prospect walks away before you even finish.

What's Wrong?

- The sale has probably been lost.
- You certainly lost your credibility.
- All the time you put into selling the prospect on a demonstration has been wasted.
- You've always thought demo was short for demolition.
- You're certainly not developing good sales habits.

Some Success Strategies:

Practice. Practice. Practice. Know the demo inside out. Backward and forward. Top to bottom. Upside down. Right side up. Well, you get the idea. Recruit others in your company to help you perfect your demo (other reps, your manager, etc.). Don't demonstrate too quickly and have answers prepared for the expected questions. Remember to highlight what the customer needs and sell the benefits of your product. Try to involve the prospect in your demo where appropriate.

#46 Pupils; Retinas; Corneas; Oh, My!

You gave a great presentation, but you looked everywhere except into the prospect's eyes.

What's Wrong?

- In not making eye contact, you seem evasive.
- The buying signals in the prospect's eyes cannot be read.
- You're lacking confidence.
- You don't know what color eyes the prospect has, but you'd recognize those wing tips anywhere.
- The prospect is not being shown any respect.

Some Success Strategies:

Make immediate eye contact with the prospect and hold it with a smile. Make that smile reach into your eyes. Understand that the eyes are the face. Well, not really. If the eyes are the face, then you're presenting to a praying mantis. The prospect hears the words emanating from your mouth, but he sees your eyes. Move your eyes, don't just stare. It's too reptilian and this often makes the prospect feel uncomfortable and edible. Maintain continual eye contact making the prospect feel important. With a group of people, your eye contact is more fleeting, as you look from person to person.

#47 Do Butterflies Have Teeth?

You're extremely nervous about presenting before two dozen top-level executives, and didn't sleep wink the night before.

What's Wrong?

- You're still new at this kind of thing.
- Perhaps you haven't rehearsed enough.
- This presentation is being taken far too seriously.
- You haven't learned how to relax.
- Well, you were finally able to fall asleep. It just happened to be during your presentation.

Some Success Strategies:

Rehearse until you know what to say backward and forward. Anticipate the questions from the audience and be prepared with clear, succinct answers. Rehearse before a mirror to study your gestures and facial expressions. See if your tongue will touch your nose. Take a deep breath before you begin the presentation. Open with a big smile and a warm greeting to "break the ice." Get the audience on your side as quickly as possible, even if they have to move their chairs. Stay loose and don't get uptight about stumbling over a word or phrase. And remember, it's just a presentation.

#48 I'd Recognize That Voice Anywhere

While trying to close a big sale, the opportunity arises to meet the prospect face-to-face, but you feel you can be just as effective with a phone call.

What's Wrong?

- It's easy for the prospect to say she has another commitment, and hang up.
- You're missing an opportunity to bond.
- Gathering useful information from other personnel is impossible if you're not there.
- As you're speaking with the prospect on the phone, your competition is sitting in her office.
- New product benefits or a demonstration can't be shared over the phone.
- You put so few miles on your company car, even the tires are beginning to rust.

Some Success Strategies:

Whenever you have the opportunity to meet with your prospect, take advantage of it. Have a game plan in place. It might be sharing information, checking the status of a sale, or meeting other influencers. Take this opportunity to make the prospect feel comfortable with you as a person, and recognize you as a business partner. The phone is also an effective sales tool, but sometimes getting before the prospect is paramount.

#49 When Four-Letter Words Kill That Four-Letter Word Called Sale!

On your first call with a prospect, you describe what you sell in very eloquent terms. You even spice up your description with four-letter words like hell, damn, and a couple of others to emphasize your position.

What's Wrong? *!@? @!!*

- You'll offend the prospect.

- This behavior reflects badly on your employer.

- You're not showing any class or professionalism.

- The prospect won't feel comfortable introducing you to others in his organization.

- The prospect certainly won't feel comfortable offering you any referrals.

- You get thrown out on your three-letter word.

Some Success Strategies:

Pick your words carefully when calling on any prospect or customer. Even if the individual swears, don't follow his lead. Never use profanity or tell risque jokes. Try a limerick instead. Keep the conversation on a professional level and present yourself in the same manner.

#50 The Good, The Bad, And The Stupid

When you travel with your sales manager, you only call on the accounts where you have wonderful relationships and all is going well. You purposely avoid the challenging accounts, the ones where you're faced with one problem after another.

What's Wrong?

☹ The expertise of your manager is not being utilized.

☹ Management is getting a false impression of the status of your business.

☹ The calls you're making aren't challenging and don't require both of you to be there.

☹ It'll come as an unpleasant surprise to management when problems with the other accounts become major and surface later.

☹ You're a good rep with a bad action plan and don't you feel *stupid* reading that here?

Some Success Strategies:

The idea is to use management in those difficult situations and not impress her with the relationships you have. Show him the problems and brainstorm together to come up with solutions. Demonstrate to him what you know and what you can do. Also use your manager's experience and learn from what he knows, does, or who he contacts to assist in resolving the issue. These are excellent opportunities to team sell and make your job easier.

#51 Maybe I Should Make It Multiple Choice

You do what any good salesperson does and ask plenty of questions when calling on a prospect, but all you're getting is one-word answers and little information.

What's Wrong?

"Yes"

✘ You're not making many sales.

✘ Closed-ended questions are being asked instead of open-ended ones.

✘ In retaliation, and to be difficult, you ask one-word questions.

✘ The prospect isn't comfortable enough to share information with you.

✘ The few open-ended questions you may be asking are not making the prospect think or speculate.

✘ You're not "earning a right" to make a follow-up call and advance the sales process.

"No"

Some Success Strategies:

After making the prospect comfortable with your presence, ask questions that elicit a thoughtful reply. You need to have a mixture of closed-ended questions that give you data and open-ended questions that give you present conditions, wants, and concerns. Ask the prospect to compare and evaluate. Have him analyze what's important and speculate on what's needed. Get him to talk about his competition and, hopefully, yours. Ask him how he "feels" about certain things; get him to express his feelings, not his corporate philosophy. Like flossing: Is it for everyone? These types of high-gain questions must also be brief, clear, and relevant to the prospect's situation and position.

Chapter 6
Handling Objections & Getting Referrals

#52 Is It The Mind That Goes First?

You made the sale and yet, after leaving the customer's office, you know you forgot something, but can't seem to remember what it was. Bewildered, you return to the office for another long afternoon of cold-calling.

What's Wrong?

? You didn't ask for any referrals.

? An opportunity to call qualified prospects is lost.

? An opportunity to use your customer's introduction is lost.

? A chance to shorten the sales cycle is lost.

? You just remembered what else you left at the customer's . . . your sales manager and now she's lost.

Some Success Strategies:

Jot down the list of things you want to accomplish during the sales call. Keep this separate from your grocery list; it's so embarrassing when you're asking the prospect about her turnips. And later, the produce manager about referrals. Ask for these referrals after the sales call has been completed. Ask even if the sale is not made. The prospect may have a legitimate reason for not doing business with you, but may know others that can use your products or services. Asking for and using referrals is a very powerful tool for any successful sales professional.

#53 But I Thought Price And Cost Were Synonyms

In sales training, you were told your products are usually priced higher than the competition's, but the client's cost will be less. You don't get it because you thought price and cost were the same thing.

What's Wrong?

$ The essence of price versus cost selling is a new concept to you.

$ If you don't get it, you'll never be able to sell it.

$ The competition will take over your territory.

$ You think two weeks in Cuba is the same as two weeks in Hawaii. Heck, they are both islands.

Some Success Strategies:

Your company's products may be priced higher but show the prospect what else you can provide. For example, focus on how your company doesn't charge for shipping and your warranty is twice that of all other bidders. Emphasize how your technical support is unparalleled in the industry. If none of this is possible, make glib small talk. When asking questions of the prospect, key in on those areas of concern where your solutions can outshine the competition. If possible, quantify these benefits. Your goal is to make the prospect realize how your products may be priced higher, but with all the extras, they'll actually cost less.

#54 Ask And Ye Shall Receive (Well, Only If Ye Have Answered Thy Objections)

You've just given a terrific presentation, but now you're not sure how to ask for the prospect's business.

What's Wrong?

- You obviously don't know how to close.

- Knowing that you don't know how to ask for the business could adversely affect your presentation.

- At this point you're a wonderful presenter, but not a salesperson.

- If you don't learn how to ask, you'll soon find yourself in Ye Olde Unemployment Line.

- If you don't ask, the answer is always "no."

Some Success Strategies:

Ask the prospect what she thinks and if she has any questions. If not, ask if there is any reason they can't do business. You can also offer the two-option close. Ask if she'd like the unit delivered on Wednesday or Friday. This is, in essence, both an effective close and a checking question. Know what close you're going to use and be comfortable using it. Practice it before a mirror or in front of a patient friend until it becomes natural. If it remains unnatural, it's probably not a good idea to use it on a prospect.

#55 Now I Have To Schedule A Seance

You've asked your customer for a referral, and she's agreed to give you one. You tell her you'll give her a call later to get that name.

What's Wrong?

- The credibility of your customer is suspect when you discover her referral has been dead for ten years.

- You didn't ask for more than one referral.

- You didn't ask the customer to actually call her contact from her office while you were there.

- You didn't ask the customer to, at least, contact the referral before you made your call.

Some Success Strategies:

Always attempt to get the customer to call the referral immediately, preferably with you present. At this point, the customer is enthusiastic about you and will do her own selling to the referral. She's also less likely to pass on anything negative. If she can't make or complete this call, be sure to take down the given name or names. Promise your customer you'll contact the referral within a week. Ask your customer to speak with the referral first so when contacted, the referral won't be caught unawares. Then be sure to follow through on your promise.

#56 Why Don't They Just Shut Up And Buy?

Objections are part of the selling process, but you'd rather not have to deal with them at all. They're an impediment, so you ignore them or pretend you don't hear them. You just keep selling!

What's Wrong?

- If you're not answering objections you won't be selling anything.
- You don't understand that objections show the prospect is interested and getting involved.
- If the prospect is ignored, they'll become irritated.
- Opportunities to uncover other needs or concerns are being missed.
- You carried on like this when you were selling cars and became the only salesperson in history to be recalled.

Some Success Strategies:

You must handle objections to sell effectively, and you begin by encouraging the prospect to open up and talk freely about his concerns. Maybe have him lie down and ask about his childhood. Continue by asking open-ended questions to obtain as much information as you can. Confirm your prospect's objection by summarizing what you've learned and reiterate it. Then you move ahead by creating an action step: prove the objection wrong, clarify what you can offer as a solution, or state what you will do next to resolve this particular objection. Your final checking question determines if the plan of action satisfies the prospect and if it does, allows you to continue.

Chapter 7

Closing The Sale

#57 And Take Your Ring Too!

You've made countless calls on a prospect and still no sale. You think he's still interested, but just unable to commit.

What's Wrong?

🔨 Other, more viable prospects are being ignored.

🔨 You don't know how to ask strong, closing questions.

🔨 It's a sickness. His office is right next to the donut shop and you can't drive by without stopping at both.

🔨 You don't know how to close.

🔨 He may not be the real decision maker.

Some Success Strategies:

Try the "walk-away" close. If you've exhausted all methods of persuading him to buy, tell him there seems to be nothing more you can do for him. Explain how your services are in need elsewhere, thank him, and "walk away." Well, because of your dual stop, it's probably "waddle away." Either the prospect calls you back to do business, or this prospect and the donut shop are no longer on your call report list.

#58 Sticks & Stones May Break My Bones, But Those Words Really Kill Me

When you use the words buy, contract, sign, or cost with your prospects you notice that many of them act fearful and reluctant to do business.

What's Wrong?

- These words intimidate.

- You sound too much like the stereotypical salesperson.

- A word like contract sounds so . . . final.

- When you say these words you have a tendency to foam at the mouth.

- Remember what your father said about signing anything? "Read the fine print first."

Some Success Strategies:

Use softer terminology that will be interpreted as you and the prospect working together. Use areas of concern rather than objections, and get their approval instead of getting them to sign. Try agreement or form instead of contract. Instead of sell or buy, how about getting them involved? Instead of totaling the car, you just got dinged . . . a lot. It's not just how you say it, it's what you say.

#59 Cross My Heart . . . Oh, You're Right, It Is On The Other Side

You're so anxious to make the sale you promise your new customer delivery dates that will be impossible to meet. Oh, what have you done?

What's Wrong?

- ♥ You just lost credibility and maybe the sale.

- ♥ There's no opportunity for future business.

- ♥ You're making unreasonable demands on your delivery people.

- ♥ This kind of thing only pays off with campaign promises.

- ♥ The reputation of your company will suffer.

Some Success Strategies:

Never make promises you can't keep. Qualify the objection as a "true" objection, and not just a smoke screen for something else. Be honest and explain to the prospect why you deliver when you do. Put a positive spin on the situation by focusing on your high quality control standards, your pre-training package, and whatever else comes to mind. If the prospect is making unreasonable demands, walk away. You'll be far better off.

#60 Etiquette & Iterate

You've had a terrific meeting and feel close to getting your prospect's business. She's asking for assistance on a number of issues, and as you flip through the notes you took, you realize some of the issues are not clear (or is it your notes?) Well, not to worry, you'll just provide what you think she wants.

What's Wrong?

➢ Assumptions are being made.

➢ You didn't synopsize the key points after the meeting.

➢ You're unable to follow up with a thank-you letter, a recap of what you covered, and a summary of action steps that will follow.

➢ Your note-taking is sloppy.

➢ Providing inappropriate solutions will damage your credibility and jeopardize the sale.

Some Success Strategies:

At the close of a major meeting, always synopsize the key issues and concerns. Be certain what is expected of you. Reiterate this in a thank-you letter and ask the prospect to contact you if there is any confusion. A thank-you letter may set you apart from the competition. Maybe add a personal touch and enclose a picture of your dog. The list of action steps shows the prospect how well you understand her position. It also transforms the verbal into reality, something now written.

#61 Is Putting His Head Between His Legs A Buying Signal?

The buyer you're talking to seems very interested in your services. He's nodding his head and seems receptive. The one thing you're not sure about is his body language; he's got both arms crossed over his midsection. But you ignore this and continue your monologue.

What's Wrong?

- You need to be a better student of body language.

- He's nodding yes, but thinking no.

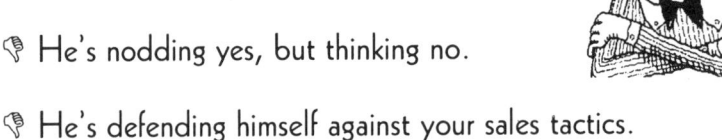

- He's defending himself against your sales tactics.

- He's desperately restraining himself from laughing out loud at your ridiculous pitch.

- The "hot button" that might make him more receptive and open-minded still hasn't been found.

Some Success Strategies:

Learn to read body language. It's easier than French and everyone speaks it. Know that crossed arms symbolize a defensive "prove it to me" attitude. A casual pose can signify a "not really interested, but I'm listening because I'm open-minded" position. If he slumps across his desk, he's either disinterested or unconscious. You must sell differently to each. Ask disarming questions and continually probe until you find the buyer's objections. Your goal is to convince the buyer to commit and become your ally.

#62 Where's A Decision Maker When You Need One?

You're excited about almost closing a sale until you're told that the person you've been selling to for the last three months isn't the final decision maker.

What's Wrong?

☺ The correct qualifying questions were not asked up front.

☺ Your prospect wanted to feel more important than she is.

☺ Now you have to determine how to get to the true decision maker.

☺ The final decision maker is the person you just hit in the parking lot.

Some Success Strategies:

It's very important at the outset to establish who's making the final decision. Focus your efforts on both meeting and satisfying the needs of this party. You may be forced to work with and through the decision maker's subordinates, but look at this as an opportunity; you'll have the chance to make another ally. And remember to send a get well card.

#63 I Know It's Just In From Paris, But It Still Makes Me Look Stupid

You make all the calls. You're seeing prospects. You're selling features. What you can't understand is why you aren't selling product.

What's Wrong?

- The benefits of your solution to the customer are being ignored.

- Customers need to have features translated into benefits.

- You haven't been trained well.

- If your product were *actually* features, you'd be having a terrific year.

- You're a great source of information, but you're not providing solutions.

Some Success Strategies:

Know the features, advantages, and benefits of your products or services (or FAB's as they are often called). Recognize that the customer enjoys the latest features, but will most often buy on how this product specifically benefits them. You must also know your advantages because of obvious competitive issues. But, focus on the benefits, benefits, benefits.

#64 What Will It Take For You To Buy This Tool Right Now, Huh, Huh, Huh!?

Though the results may not show it, you're excited about selling and you know you're doing all the right things. You're working extremely hard on your close, perhaps to where your behavior may be construed as too aggressive.

What's Wrong?

🖐 Prospective customers are being turned off.

🖐 You're not convincing the prospect to buy, you're forcing the prospect to see it your way.

🖐 This approach will make getting referral business difficult.

🖐 Your aggressive demeanor will alienate you from your co-workers.

🖐 It's probably not a good idea for you to sell chain saws.

Some Success Strategies:

Work at changing your selling style. Soften your approach and ask more open-ended questions of the prospect. Adjust your technique to each buyer, don't just offer a standard "pitch" which in itself, can irritate people. Be more observant when addressing a prospect and watch, and then adjust, for a negative reaction. Watching them running in the opposite direction should be construed as negative. If you can't determine where, exactly, you're going wrong, ask your manager or one of your associates to critique your style.

#65 All I Asked For Was Two Front Teeth

You've qualified the prospect, uncovered her needs, offered solutions, and left it up to her to order. You can't understand why she went with a competitor.

What's Wrong?

- You never asked for the order.
- Your competitor did.
- You're afraid of rejection.
- You still believe in the tooth fairy.
- The various closing techniques are foreign to you.
- Hoping, wishing, and praying for the order usually doesn't work.

Some Success Strategies:

Many prospects will expect you to ask them for an order. Unless they acknowledge the purchase, always incorporate asking for the order into the closing process. Ask checking questions to determine when and if asking for the order is appropriate. Walk away knowing where you stand; either you have the business or you know the objection for why you're not getting it. And it probably never hurts to wear your lucky suit.

#66 Making A List And Checking It Twice

You're trying to close a sale with a prospect, but your competition happens to be selling at a much better price. Your solution offers other benefits, both tangible and intangible, but instead of presenting the benefits, you make the prospect guess what they are.

What's Wrong?

✓ You're not sure how to present the benefits of your solution.

✓ This indecisiveness could translate into no sale.

✓ This obstacle will be recurring if you don't resolve it.

✓ All your benefits will mean nothing if you can't help the prospect see their value.

✓ You're obviously inexperienced.

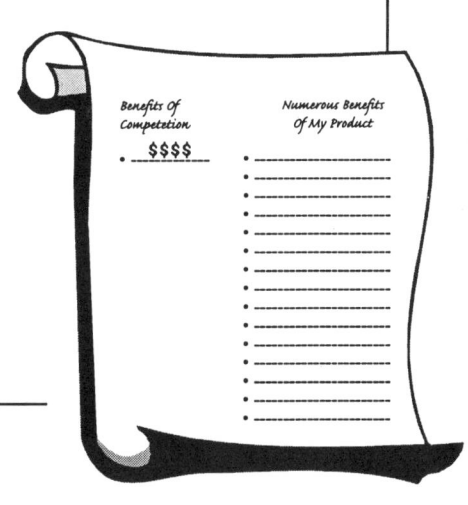

Some Success Strategies:

You need to demonstrate to the prospect the strength of your proposal. List, in two adjacent columns, the benefits of selecting the competition versus selecting yours. The column for the competition will have one line item—price. Your column will consist of numerous benefits. Thousands, if possible. The discrepancy between the two columns should be most obvious to the decision-maker. This is a great tool for alerting the prospect to your true value.

#67 Tell Him I'm Out And Moved To Brazil

You're so anxious to find out if you've got the business you call the prospect every other day. The prospect has stopped taking your calls and his secretary says he left the country.

What's Wrong?

🌴 You're acting very desperate.

🌴 The sale is being jeopardized with your annoying calls.

🌴 This behavior is extremely unprofessional.

🌴 Keep it up and you won't have any customers.

🌴 You just discovered that nonrefundable plane ticket you bought to Rio won't fly on your expense report.

Some Success Strategies:

During the sales call, you should ask when a decision will be made. If that time frame is extended, contact the account and check on the status of the decision. Probe to see if there might be any concerns that might not have been identified initially. See if any more information is needed. Offer yourself as a partner in solving their problem.

Chapter 8
After The Sale & After The Call

#68 Sold: Going, Going, Gone . . .

The prospect has become a customer and you immediately move on, wasting little time on post-sale follow-up. Their new system may be a little complex, but they can train themselves with your terrific manuals. And you'll give them a call in a few weeks.

What's Wrong?

- The sale is only part of the selling process and you still don't realize this.

- Your customer could become a dissatisfied customer and return your "solution."

- Much of your time will be spent answering questions and handling complaints if the customer's not trained properly.

- You could be given the trainer's responsibilities and discover 101 *other* stupid things to sabotage your business.

- Opportunity for future business will be nil.

Some Success Strategies:

Dedicate time for training and follow-up with your new customer. Be sure they're comfortable with the solution you've provided. Check up on them periodically to be certain they're realizing all the benefits of your service or products. Remember to ask your latest satisfied customer for referrals. You also want them to come back to you when they need upgrades, and maybe, something new. Remember, not unlike a marriage, you're not just closing a sale, you're opening a relationship.

#69 When No Follow-Up Is A Foul Up

You're doing a terrific job developing leads and making sales calls. You're so busy, you forget to follow-up with your prospects.

What's Wrong?

🏵 Without prompt follow-up, the prospect will lose interest.

🏵 You're disorganized.

🏵 No follow-up gives you no reason to see the prospect again.

🏵 Future sales will be hurt.

🏵 You just remembered dropping the cat off at the vets for a check-up four years ago.

Some Success Strategies:

If the prospect asks for something and you can provide it, do so immediately. Show them how much they mean to you and that doesn't mean sending a mushy greeting card. You also want a good reason to get in front of your future client again, thus advancing the sales process. Organize your day more effectively, leaving time for follow-up.

#70 I Shall Return (Except Not During Office Hours)

During the first sales call, you covered everything so completely that you left yourself no reason to go back. And you didn't get the sale. Undeterred you keep on selling, er, meeting prospects.

What's Wrong?

- You've collected more business cards than anyone in the country, but you're not getting paid for that.

- Any opportunity to continue bonding and selling with the prospect is gone.

- You don't understand the multi-call sales process.

- Without a return call, you won't have the opportunity to find out what the competition is doing.

- You're obviously offering off-the-shelf solutions, not something customized to the prospect's needs.

Some Success Strategies:

Always plan on returning to a good prospect. Encourage the prospect to want to see you again. Suggest what you can do to save his money, get that promotion, understand photosynthesis, etc. But, don't be too specific. You need time to craft the right sales solution. You also need time to find out, through this bonding process, what the competition may be offering.

#71 Heads You Pay, Tails We Split It

You take a major client out to lunch to celebrate your new business partnership. You order first and just order a salad, and tell your new customer to order anything on the menu. You're just having a salad because your company is trying to watch expenses.

What's Wrong?

- You should not have ordered first.

- You should have chosen the restaurant.

- It makes your company look like it's not doing well.

- The customer may feel you're going to cut corners on supporting his business.

- You warn him the servings are huge, and suggest he order off the children's menu.

Some Success Strategies:

Don't restrict a customer or prospect from ordering whatever they want off a menu. If there are limitations to your expense budget, choose a restaurant within that price range. Don't discuss negative financials with a prospect or new client. It will only serve to intimidate them. And, the courteous thing to do is allow the customer to order first. If he chooses not to for some reason, and you only feel like a salad, reassure him that you're not hungry. Remember to say this loudly enough to cover the roar of your stomach.

#72 Elevators Have Ears Too

After making a sales call you're sharing your thoughts with your manager on the elevator as you leave. There are four strangers with you, but it doesn't stop you from telling your boss how this account might be a complete waste of time and the guy you just met with is a "complete idiot."

What's Wrong?

- Any one of these strangers could work for the company you just left.

- Your manager didn't stop you before you said too much.

- The guy behind you is the complete idiot's brother, the "complete tattletale."

- Analyzing a sales call or criticizing a prospect on the prospect's premises is just plain stupid.

Some Success Strategies:

Don't voice your thoughts on any elevator. Everyone there is just listening for an alternative to Muzak. Share thoughts with your manager when it's just the two of you. Follow the same strategy when eating in restaurants or other public places proximate to the business; it's an amazingly small world. You don't want a careless remark ruining a possible sale.

#73 And I Even Took Her To Lunch!

You're really upset that your competitor won the business. You're so angry you never want to talk to that unappreciative ex-prospect again!

What's Wrong?

- This reaction is not good for your health.

- If you don't follow-up with the prospect you won't know why you lost the business.

- There might be other business on the table that you could secure, but you'll never know about it.

- The opportunity to secure future business will be lost.

- Now it's too late to cancel that e-mail you sent where you criticize your ex-prospect.

Some Success Strategies:

Maintain a positive relationship with your competitor's new client. Learn where you failed and your competitor succeeded. Show you still care about her and her business. Determine if there might be another area in which you can offer assistance. Maybe show her how to disco. Be cognizant of future possibilities and use this individual for referrals. Always talk out your frustrations and anger with friends or loved ones.

#74 Do Partners Need Pre-Nuptial Agreements?

You love selling the term "partners" to your prospects, but after securing the sale you seem to forget just what this word means. Now you're finding that these "partners" are reordering with the competition and won't return your phone calls.

What's Wrong?

- Your credibility and integrity have been severely damaged.

- The relationships you worked so hard to build have been torn apart.

- This job is much more difficult if you're not taking advantage of repeat sales.

- Future business will be tough to get since your reputation will precede you.

- The same thing is happening in your personal life as another tennis partner left you to play singles.

Some Success Strategies:

If you're going to talk partnership, then treat your customer like a real partner. Try conducting regular business reviews with the customer to be certain there are no concerns. Determine what you might be able to improve upon. Work with as many people in the organization as possible to better understand your customer. Think strategically with your partner and also provide them with a means for evaluating your relationship. This creates a tool for improvement, tracks quality, and demonstrates your integrity.

#75 Should It Be Sincerely, Regards, Or Hugs And Kisses?

You have no idea when you should or should not send out thank-you notes to prospects and customers. Stupidly you just don't bother.

What's Wrong?

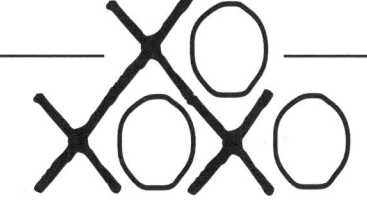

✘ You're neglecting a professional courtesy.

✘ If your competition does send a note, then they'll have an advantage.

✘ If your competition doesn't send a note, then you've just missed an opportunity to gain an edge.

✘ You're missing an opportunity to reiterate your interest in the business and, perhaps, add something of value that was left out in your earlier meeting.

✘ The last time you sent out a batch of thank-you notes, you actually signed them "Hugs and Kisses."

Some Success Strategies:

Write the thank-you notes and make them simple, clear, and to the point. Have different ones available for different contacts: telephone, in-person, post-demonstration, after a purchase, after a referral, after meeting him on the street, and even on an anniversary. Send a thank-you note to the prospect that purchased from someone else too. In sales, little things mean a lot. A personalized thank-you note is one of those little things that becomes a big thing.

Chapter 9

Your Image & Doing The Right Thing

#76 First Impressions

When meeting and shaking hands with a prospect for the first time you both notice a huge, yellow stain on your sleeve.

What's Wrong?

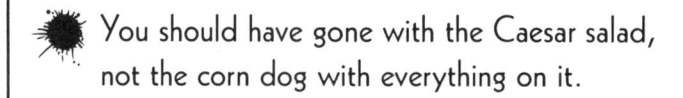

- You should have gone with the Caesar salad, not the corn dog with everything on it.
- You look like a slob.
- The prospect wonders why you don't care enough to look your best for this meeting.
- You missed this one in the "Supervisors" book.
- The selling skills will have to be magnificent to overcome this fashion faux pas.

Some Success Strategies:

If you've reached this point, try to make light of the stain; maybe ask if the prospect has something you can smear on the other sleeve. Otherwise, apologize for what looks like a mustard mishap. Don't ignore it or the prospect may think you always dress with condiments. Try to always check your appearance before a sales call.

#77 Send In The Clowns

You frequently wear outfits that aren't color coordinated, accessorize with jewelry that is garish and ridiculous-looking, and even wear silly looking shoes.

What's Wrong?

- You don't look professional.

- This image reflects poorly on your company.

- Kids come up and squeeze your big, red nose . . . and it's real!

- If this is the attention you pay to your dress, what attention can you give to a client?

- Prospects will be embarrassed to be seen with you, and heck, your own management will be embarrassed.

Some Success Strategies:

Have someone help you shop if you're fashion-challenged, and if you know them well enough, they can help you dress too. Check out the fashion magazines and read books on dressing for business. Compare yourself to others in your profession. If there's a question about jewelry, simply don't wear it. Never dress in the dark. If you still can't change your odd dressing habits, become something else. Like a teenager.

#78 A Group Photo Of Myself

The sales team is just that, a team. But, you'd rather make the sale on your own. You think you can do just fine without your support associates.

What's Wrong?

☆ You've got a big ego.

☆ You'll alienate your sales partners.

☆ The prospect won't feel as important being supported by one versus a team.

☆ Closing the sale will be more difficult.

☆ When you do need help from your teammates, you won't be able to get it.

☆ You even quit the basketball team in school because you had to play with others.

Some Success Strategies:

Recognize the strength of your team and the attributes of each player. Use your team and delegate, allowing you to sell more effectively. A complex sale, or ongoing multiple sales, require the skills of many specialists: sales, technical, training, etc. Sell these components to your prospect as an advantage to them. They'll be flattered and more comfortable with their buying decision.

#79 Lunch On The Rocks, Please

You insist on having a couple of drinks with a potential customer at lunch. It loosens you up. It also makes you loud, obnoxious, and an embarrassment.

What's Wrong?

- You're showing no respect for the prospect.
- You're showing no respect for your employer.
- It's a bad habit that can only get worse.
- Keep it up and you'll be toasting a new opportunity.
- Drinking may cloud your business judgment.
- What kind of impression are you making doing a dance with a salad bowl on your head and bread sticks in your ears?

Some Success Strategies:

Simply stay away from the liquor. You can't stop your companion from drinking, but you don't have to indulge. Dinner can be a different story, but lunch beverages should include nothing stronger than an artificial sweetener. If you need to loosen up, try lumbar twists in the lobby. If your prospect orders you a drink, thank them and leave it on the table—untouched. It's O.K. not to drink.

#80 He Orders 20 Lots And You Get 20 Years

A difficult buyer you've been wooing for months is beginning to soften, but he's suggesting he'll only buy if you help him out. He's talking kickbacks or payoffs and you're starting to think about it.

What's Wrong?

- It's illegal. And unethical.
- You'll be irreparably damaging the reputation of your company.
- You'll never be able to trust the buyer.
- What kind of business will you do when a new buyer is hired?
- You've got a new sales manager. You call him Warden.
- Any values you might have will be instantly compromised.

Some Success Strategies:

Be honest and never do business under the table. Unless, of course, you're selling flooring. If this kind of questionable situation arises, consult with your manager. Never put yourself in a position where your principles or the reputation of your company are compromised. When selling in foreign countries, be aware that this sort of practice is fairly common. Explain up front that your company does not permit this sort of business practice and you must respect the integrity of your company. If this causes you to lose the sale, accept the loss. Share the information with your manager and take a tour of the local sights. Don't forget to take pictures as it's likely you'll not be coming back.

#81 Talk, Talk, Talk And Watch The Order Walk

Without even realizing it you sold your prospect. But, you continued to talk so much through your closing that you actually oversold. And now the prospect isn't so sure she wants to buy.

What's Wrong?

- 😐 You though you were being paid by the syllable.

- 😐 You might have talked your way out of the sale.

- 😐 During the sales close you don't know when to close your mouth.

- 😐 You weren't really observing or listening to the prospect for buying signals.

- 😐 The prospect is confused, and probably angry, at seemingly being manipulated.

Some Success Strategies:

Watch for buying signals and then ask for the order. If the prospect becomes a customer, then say no more about features, advantages, and benefits. Focus on the customer needs, don't prattle on about nonessentials. Save that for your spouse. Have a rough script in mind when presenting so you're less likely to stray off-course.

#82 Kiss, Bow, or Shake Hands?

Because of sales opportunities in other countries, you're beginning to travel around the world. Unknowingly, you're not treating and selling to customers in Asia differently than those you've sold to for so long in New York City.

What's Wrong?

- You're going to encounter resistance in Asia.

- Different cultures demand different selling approaches.

- Your sales results from region to region will be tremendously erratic.

- You'll never elevate yourself beyond a local sales position.

- You get so confused about the local customs that you end up kissing your prospect on the top of his head as he bows to greet you.

Some Success Strategies:

Learn the ways people around the world talk, act, and make decisions. Be culture sensitive. Spend time learning about unfamiliar regions of the world with an experienced associate. Ask questions of the citizenry. Read about this new part of the world and research it like you would a new prospect. Show restraint and respect. Learn how to use chopsticks—for eating, not drumming.

#83 As Simple As 1-2-4

Your latest business opportunity has you juggling several issues demanding different solutions. You're also meeting numerous influencers and decision makers that are asking for support. Even though you're having problems keeping this all straight, it's exhilarating just "flying by the seat of your pants."

What's Wrong?

○ This is a complex sale, and you're not treating it like one.

○ You're not taking the time to plot a course of action.

○ With so many players you could be losing the sale, and not even know it until it's too late.

○ The team sales approach is not being utilized.

○ Other business is being neglected because of all the time you spend on this project.

Some Success Strategies:

When the sale becomes complicated, take the time to analyze the process. List the influencers and decision makers by importance and enumerate the key issues. Determine where you can best "team sell" with your associates. Develop an action plan with a timeline for goal setting. Recognize when you need help and don't be afraid to ask for it and never lose sight of your objective.

#84 I Know! I Know! I Know! Well, Maybe I Don't!

Being anxious to satisfy the customer has you telling her everything she wants to know. Except that much of what you're telling you're really not sure about.

What's Wrong?

- ☹ You're trying too hard.

- ☹ The customer will become upset when you come back to her and her expectations have to be altered.

- ☹ Your credibility is suspect.

- ☹ This reminds you, a little, of when you were that attention-starved, annoying kid in grade school that always had his hand up yet never had the slightest idea what the answer was.

- ☹ Management will be displeased by you deluding the customer and also misrepresenting your capabilities.

Some Success Strategies:

Listen to the customer and understand exactly what they're asking. Don't offer an instant remedy and study all the possible ramifications. Enlist the aid of your co-workers (team) to offer the best solution. Tell your customer you'll get back with her once you've had the opportunity to better determine which direction is the most cost-effective, least time consuming, most ego gratifying, etc. The prospect will appreciate you taking the time to look after her best interests.

#85 Undress For Success

You're calling on businesses in a market where all your prospects and customers dress very casually, no suits or ties. Conversely, when calling on these people you tend to always wear an expensive suit, smile even when you don't feel like it, and yet wonder why they don't warm up to you.

What's Wrong?

- The people you're calling on are intimidated.

- You seem smug and pretentious.

- You're not adapting to the marketplace.

- There are no relationships being cultivated between you and the business people in your territory.

- It's probably those silly suspenders. The people you're calling on actually wear them to hold up their pants.

Some Success Strategies:

In trying to relate to the customer, dress a bit more like the customer. You might shed the suit for a sport coat and slacks, or even take off the coat for certain accounts. It's important you don't be perceived as a threat or a buffoon. The opposite also applies if selling in a cosmopolitan environment, and you're accustomed to dressing a bit more casually. Here you stop whittling, and get rid of the banjo and chewing tobacco. It's time to upgrade your wardrobe. It's far easier to become credible, gain confidences, and establish rapport when you fit in.

#86 Questions? Not Me, I'm Selling!

You know you're supposed to ask questions on a sales call, but you're not sure what direction these questions should take. You feel better if you just let the prospect begin and then you try to close when you see an opening.

What's Wrong?

- The prospect will be controlling the call, not you.

- Significant issues will not be covered if you don't ask the right questions.

- You'll irritate your prospect by attempting to close at an inappropriate time.

- After three months of this you're asking questions like, "What's a commission check?" and "Is There Life After Not Selling?"

Some Success Strategies:

Attempt to remember a basic questioning format. Start broad, and then get specific. Build your questions from previous prospect responses and try to keep them simple. This sets up direct, easy-to-understand answers. Remember that sensitive questions demand a relevant explanation. Always be probing for prospect needs and a means of satisfying them. And remember, this probing stuff should only be attempted by sales professionals.

Chapter 10

Time Management & Goal Setting

#87 Cleveland At Ten, Seattle At Two

After making a call in the morning, you have to drive two hundred miles for your second appointment, and then you're on the road two more hours to get to your third.

What's Wrong?

- Too much time behind the windshield.

- This is poor territory management.

- This is poor territory alignment.

- You have more speeding tickets than business cards.

- There's tremendous wear and tear on the automobile—and on you.

- By the last call you're tired, and you can't give your best to the customer.

Some Success Strategies:

Whenever possible, schedule your appointments in a tight geographical area. If there are too many miles between your accounts, discuss realignment with your manager. See if flying between cities makes financial sense. Use the phone more effectively, eliminating the need for some physical calls. Your company might consider hiring someone to assist you in the outlying communities. Consider jetpooling.

#88 Should I Or Shouldn't I Use A Comma?

You're spending a lot of your valuable time on petty details and you simply cannot find the time to get in front of the customer.

What's Wrong?

- You wrote a grammatically perfect memo on washing your hands before you eat.

- There is no selling here.

- You're not using your time efficiently.

- Prioritizing is a definite problem.

- Your sales manager won't be pleased with your sales results.

Some Success Strategies:

Do the petty "stuff" after hours or when you can't be making sales calls. If the customer requires extra attention and you simply can't find the time, ask management for assistance. No matter what the problem, your manager can be trusted to take them out to play golf. Utilize customer service. Try to do all your detail work at once, perhaps setting aside one or two evenings a week. Take a course on time management and learn how to prioritize.

#89 Look Who Drove Up. Quick, Put Up The "Gone Fishin' " Sign!

You're seeing customers that really don't have anything new to discuss with you. And, you're not doing anything for them that makes the trip worthwhile either.

What's Wrong?

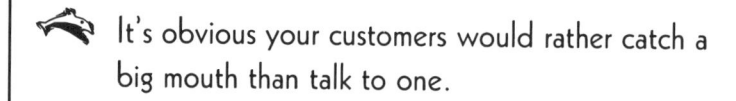

- It's obvious your customers would rather catch a big mouth than talk to one.
- The customer's time is being wasted.
- You don't like using a phone, a fax, FedEx, or UPS.
- This is poor territory management.
- This is no way to grow your business.

Some Success Strategies:

You need to utilize today's communication tools whenever possible. Cover what business you can over the phone. Determine if using the Internet is an option. Only see customers if there's a real need: new product introduction, problems, more training, bonding, an Elvis sighting, etc.

#90 And I Don't Even Own Stock In The Phone Company!

Too much time is being spent on the phone, and you don't know how to cut back. You know you need to get out and see more of your prospects and customers face-to-face but can't seem to break the phone habit.

What's Wrong?

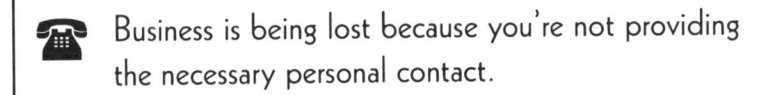

- ☎ Nothing's wrong with spending this much time on the phone if you're a teenage girl.

- ☎ Business is being lost because you're not providing the necessary personal contact.

- ☎ You're not communicating at all with those people who never pick up the phone.

- ☎ Management wants you in front of the customer whenever possible.

Some Success Strategies:

Write down objectives for each phone call and stick to them. Make and receive calls at the same time every day and set specific time limits. Let your customers know when you're available for them to call you. Utilize effective, but polite exit lines when necessary. If you're caught in conversation with someone who babbles endlessly; just let your manager know you have to go. You'll call her back tomorrow.

#91 Pride Goeth Before The No Sale

You work for a large organization with many divisions and you're having a problem gaining access to a major account. You know one of your associates in another division has a good relationship with someone at this account, but you prefer to try to make inroads on your own.

What's Wrong?

♦ Your favorite game is solitaire.

♦ Pride is forcing you to waste a favorable introduction and referral.

♦ Existing relationships developed in sister divisions are not being exploited.

♦ You're wasting your company resources by working a path already traveled.

♦ You're also missing opportunities to team sell with your sales associates.

Some Success Strategies:

Take advantage of your organization's depth and diversity. Utilize any means possible to gain access to the prospect. Never forget groveling. Attend cross-divisional meetings and exchange information on key accounts. Share data on those doing business with you now, but accent those key accounts you're after. If there is an opportunity, determine if your associate is in a position to introduce you and your services. You might make a joint sales call to show the variety of resources available to the client. Your mission is to get the names, get the introductions, and get inside!

#92 Not Another Bull In A China Shop!

You're focused on your job and not thinking about any specific goals. You're just going to make quota, and no one's going to stop you!

What's Wrong?

- If you don't have any goals, you won't know where you're going. And if you don't know where you're going, any path will take you there.

- Without long range goals you'll miss the greater opportunities with your customers and prospects.

- You'll miss the opportunities that might exist within your own organization.

- Without goals, your sales job will become tiresome and boring and tedious and repetitious . . .

Some Success Strategies:

It's important that you establish goals, not just to define your job but also to define your potential. If you're ambitious, you'll need more than just a monthly or yearly quota to stay driven. Create a three-year plan and work with your manager to determine if it's realistic. Ask yourself where you want to be in five years. Set goals for cracking a select number of major accounts, selling a new product, or making a high number of cold calls. Reward yourself for attaining these goals. Maybe take a trip around the world. Management may not recognize your personal goals, but that's no reason why you can't. Give yourself something to strive for on both a short-term and long-term basis.

Chapter 11

Other Stupid Stuff

#93 The Rocky Road (With Two Scoops) I Can Handle

It's been a miserable day of one rejection after another. To you, it qualifies as a complete failure. You're thinking of going back to the ice cream shop, and giving up on sales.

What's Wrong?

- Learning how to use rejection as a springboard to sales success is still something new for you.
- Your self-confidence is nonexistent.
- Perseverance is a word you have to look up.
- Your motivation is in the same place as your confidence.
- Your butterfat content is too low.

Some Success Strategies:

Think back and see if you can determine why you were rejected and learn from it. You might even try to laugh about the experience. Continue to hone your selling skills. Look at sales as a numbers game, a game of averages. You make more calls, you receive more rejections, and you close more sales. Remember, they're not saying "no" to you, they're saying "no" to your product or service. Of course, a double scoop of fudge ripple will make a tough day easier to swallow.

#94 Sorry, I'm A Day Late, But It's Not My Fault

You're consistently late for appointments. You can't seem to help it, and you're beginning to think it's genetic. After all, you were born three weeks late.

What's Wrong?

- You were a big baby. And still are acting like one.
- One of your weaknesses is scheduling.
- You don't value the prospect's time.
- These appointments are not being taken seriously.
- You're losing credibility.
- The competition could be taking advantage of your tardiness.

Some Success Strategies:

Being late occasionally is unavoidable. If you're running behind schedule, call and let your prospect know and see if it's okay to meet later. Show respect for the prospect's time. Schedule your locating of the building, driving time, parking, etc. so you'll arrive early. Send a birthday card to your mother. Make sure it's not belated.

#95 Been There, Done That

There's nothing in sales you haven't experienced or learned. You don't need any more classes to improve your skills, and you've sworn never to listen to another selling or personal growth audio cassette.

What's Wrong?

- This is very close-minded and arrogant behavior.

- Management finds you very difficult to supervise.

- You don't recognize the difference in selling yesterday versus today.

- Your own associates will find you insufferable.

- You haven't sold a thing in months, and the closest you've come to a date is at the grocery store when you passed them to get to the prunes.

Some Success Strategies:

Be very open-minded. Look at the different selling techniques available in the market and see if any can be adapted to your style. Examine new communication tools to help make you more efficient. Take company classes to improve your understanding of emerging sales tactics, like team selling for complex accounts. Take business classes to assist you in learning more about the actual "business" of your clients. Sales is very dynamic, and you just can't know everything.

#96 Oh, My Aching Back!

Oh, how you hate trade shows. You take any opportunity you can to leave your booth and wander outside the hall, talk with other vendors, and even sneak back up to your room for a peek at the TV.

What's Wrong?

☠ Some customers will resent the fact you're not in the booth when they come around.

☠ You're missing the opportunity to save a tremendous amount of time, effort, and money by having all these prospects and customers come to you, instead of you having to go to them.

☠ It reflects poorly on your company when your booth is left unattended.

☠ You're wasting the substantial monies your company has paid to participate in this show.

☠ You get hooked on a soap opera.

Some Success Strategies:

Take breaks only when necessary and when the show slows down. Do stretching exercises to ease the pressure on your back from all the standing. If the back really gets tight, hang upside down and greet people from this position. It'll be an attention getter. And greet everyone that passes, each could be a potential client. Even if they don't become a customer, they might still expand your industry knowledge base, and perhaps, offer some insight about your competition. Set up appointments ahead of time with prospects you know will be there to take advantage of this opportunity to meet.

#97 Aloha, Job!

You've just returned from a sales incentive trip with your company and you and your spouse had a wonderful time. You might have had a bit too much to drink on a couple of occasions, and you can't remember exactly what you said to the CEO that last night, but heck, everybody else laughed!

What's Wrong?

- You were immature and irresponsible.

- Upper management was not favorably impressed.

- You can't appreciate the trip if you can't remember parts of it.

- Your career may be beached.

- During the luau, and after too many Mai Tais, you pointed out the many similarities between your absent sales manager and the main course.

Some Success Strategies:

Be cognizant that any kind of a group business trip will place you under the corporate microscope. If you're interested in gaining greater responsibility or moving into management, then act responsibly. Have fun, but don't overdo it. Restrain from any eccentric behavior. Don't be boorish or outrageous in your manner or speech. Don't bring up politics, religion, or what you were in a previous life. This goes for your spouse too. Put yourself in management's position and ask if you'd want to work side-by-side with an embarrassment. Remember aloha doesn't only mean hello. It also means good-bye.

#98 I Cannot Tell A Lie, Except On My Expense Report

In looking to make a little extra spending money, you pad your expense report. It's not a big deal, but you file false charges for about $30 a month.

What's Wrong?

- It's unethical (and illegal) behavior.

- If discovered, you could lose your job.

- This might just be the stepping stone to bigger and more deceitful things.

- Your conscience will take a beating. Hopefully.

- Now you're carrying it too far. You just sold your company car.

Some Success Strategies:

Cheating on your expenses cannot be justified. Even if everybody's doing it, that doesn't mean you have to join the club. Be truthful to your employer and to yourself. Never allow money to take precedent over ethical and moral actions. You'll be recognized for your honest contributions to the company, but you'll be *ostracized* for any dishonesty. And you don't want to spend the rest of your life with your head in the ground.

#99 Maybe I Should Just Be A Sales Manager

It's been so tough you haven't been able to make an appointment in weeks, let alone a sale, and you're questioning whether sales is right for you. You enjoy the profession, but a number of associates have made a list of characteristics that a top salesperson should have and you don't have any of them. So you made an appointment with a job recruiter.

What's Wrong?

- ☑ Perhaps your associates see you as competition and want you gone.

- ☑ Giving up is not a good trait for a successful salesperson.

- ☑ It isn't always characteristics that make a top salesperson.

- ☑ You haven't taken the time to examine your work habits to see if improvement can be made.

- ☑ The job recruiter even stood you up.

Some Success Strategies:

All salespeople go through tough stretches. That's normal. Use this time to examine how you're doing your business. Look for help from your sales manager. Though salespeople have many unique characteristics, there are some common traits that many experts feel are necessary to be successful. Be proactive, enthusiastic, communicate well, and be an expert in your field. Build personal relationships and never stop networking. Remember the five-foot rule. If you don't, then you're skimming this book. If you don't have any of these traits and you're not interested in developing them, then maybe it's time to look elsewhere. You might want to look at marketing.

#100 Is That A Participle Dangling From Your Gerund?

You feel confident writing sales letters and yet your response rate is poor. You're sure it's just a numbers game so you're not going to change a thing. You'll just keep on writing.

What's Wrong?

- It could be a poorly composed letter and that'll close the door on ever making contact with the prospect.

- You're not even making the effort to determine if you're going about it the wrong way.

- You're not spending enough time in front of the prospect, but you are spending too much time behind the desk.

- Close-mindedness is not a good trait for a salesperson.

- It could have something to do with the fact that you've never learned the whole alphabet.

Some Success Strategies:

Begin by thanking the prospect for his interest and then state your purpose. Be clear and specific and highlight the benefits of your service to the prospect. Be aggressive in your close by asking him to call you, or if he's busy, let him know you'll be contacting him by a specified date. Conclude with another line of appreciation. Your letter should be tightly written, well-punctuated, and should have no misspellings. Write it, rewrite it, and then rewrite it again. Then have your fifth grade English teacher check it over.

#101 I'm Finished Washing Your Car Boss, Anything Else?

It's important for you to please your sales manager. Some people contend you're going overboard, but you know they're just jealous of the relationship you've cultivated.

What's Wrong?

- ☒ You'll alienate your sales associates.

- ☒ The sales manager may condone your fawning behavior, but not respect you.

- ☒ After washing her car, she'll insist that you wax it.

- ☒ If your sales manager leaves you could be in a difficult position.

- ☒ In working so hard to satisfy the manager and her personal agenda, you're neglecting your territory.

- ☒ You could be wrongly promoted on the basis of your relationship and not your abilities.

Some Success Strategies:

It's important you nurture a strong relationship with your manager, but that relationship should not be open to misinterpretation. Respond to the wishes of management, but, even though it sounds corny, be true to yourself. Keep the relationship on a business level and always be a professional. You want to maintain your integrity and advance on the merits of your accomplishments. Of course, it doesn't hurt to remember her birthday with a little something. Maybe her anniversary too. And Christmas . . . and the 4th of July . . . and Groundhog Day . . .

Summary

Listen. This word is the most powerful tool in sales today. Well, it always has been, but we often forget because we have our own stories to tell.

Ask yourself if you've done any of the stupid things in this book. You probably have, but that's okay. It shows you're not living in a closet.

So you're still selling every day of your life, in one form or another. And that's exciting. But remember to look again at the success strategies and see if they can offer some help. We think they can.

Good luck and happy selling!

About The Publisher

Richard Chang Associates, Inc. is a diversified organizational improvement consulting, training, and publishing firm based in Irvine, California. They provide a wide range of products and services to organizations worldwide in the areas of organizational development, quality improvement, team performance, and learning systems. The Publications Division of Richard Chang Associates, Inc., established to provide individuals with a wide variety of practical resources for continuous learning in the workplace or on a personal level, is pleased to bring you this book.

RICHARD CHANG ASSOCIATES

Richard Chang Associates, Inc.
Publications Division
15265 Alton Parkway, Suite 300
Irvine, CA 92618
(800) 756-8096   (714) 727-7477
Fax: (714) 727-7007
www.richardchangassociates.com

Additional Resources From Richard Chang Associates, Inc. Publications Division

Practical Guidebook Collection

Quality Improvement Series

Continuous Process Improvement
Continuous Improvement Tools, Volume 1
Continuous Improvement Tools, Volume 2
Step-By-Step Problem Solving
Meetings That Work!
Improving Through Benchmarking
Succeeding As A Self-Managed Team
Satisfying Internal Customers First!
Process Reengineering In Action
Measuring Organizational Improvement Impact

Management Skills Series

Coaching Through Effective Feedback
Expanding Leadership Impact
Mastering Change Management
On-The-Job Orientation And Training
Re-Creating Teams During Transitions
Planning Successful Employee Performance
Coaching For Peak Employee Performance
Evaluating Employee Performance
Interviewing And Selecting High Performers

High-Impact Training Series

Creating High-Impact Training
Identifying Targeted Training Needs
Mapping A Winning Training Approach
Producing High-Impact Learning Tools
Applying Successful Training Techniques
Measuring The Impact Of Training
Make Your Training Results Last

Workplace Diversity Series

Capitalizing On Workplace Diversity
Successful Staffing In A Diverse Workplace
Team Building For Diverse Work Groups
Communicating In A Diverse Workplace
Tools For Valuing Diversity

High Performance Team Series

Success Through Teamwork
Building A Dynamic Team
Measuring Team Performance
Team Decision-Making Techniques

Guidebooks are also available in fine bookstores.

Additional Resources From Richard Chang Associates, Inc. Publications Division

Personal Growth And Development Collection
Managing Your Career in a Changing Workplace
Unlocking Your Career Potential
Marketing Yourself and Your Career
Making Career Transitions

101 Stupid Things Series
101 Stupid Things Trainers Do To Sabotage Success
101 Stupid Things Supervisors Do To Sabotage Success
101 Stupid Things Salespeople Do To Sabotage Success
101 Stupid Things Business Travelers Do To Sabotage Success
101 Stupid Things Employees Do To Sabotage Success

Training Products
Step-By-Step Problem Solving TOOLKIT™
Meetings That Work! Practical Guidebook TOOLPAK™
Continuous Improvement Tools, Volume 1 Practical Guidebook TOOLPAK™

Packaged Training Programs
High Involvement Teamwork™
Continuous Process Improvement

Videotapes
Mastering Change Management**
Quality: You Don't Have To Be Sick To Get Better*
Achieving Results Through Quality Improvement*
Total Quality: Myths, Methods, Or Miracles**
   Featuring Drs. Ken Blanchard and Richard Chang
Empowering The Quality Effort**
   Featuring Drs. Ken Blanchard and Richard Chang
Optimizing Customer Value*
   Featuring Richard Chang
Creating High-Impact Training*
   Featuring Richard Chang

Total Quality Video Series And Workbooks
Building Commitment**
Teaming Up**
Applied Problem Solving**
Self-Directed Evaluation**

* Produced by American Media Inc.   ** Produced by Double Vision Studios